D1410677

Everything You Need to Know About

BODY DYSMORPHIC DISORDER

Dealing with a Distorted Body Image

Learning about body dysmorphic disorder is the first step to dealing with this difficult problem.

• THE NEED TO KNOW LIBRARY •

Everything You Need to Know About

BODY DYSMORPHIC DISORDER

Dealing with a Distorted Body Image

Pamela Walker

THE ROSEN PUBLISHING GROUP, INC.
NEW YORK

Published in 1999 by The Rosen Publishing Group, Inc.
29 East 21st Street, New York, NY 10010

First Edition

Library of Congress Cataloging-in-Publication Data

Walker, Pamela
    Everything you need to know about body dysmorphic disorder / by Pamela Walker.
        p.   cm. — (The need to know library)
    Includes bibliographical references and index.
    Summary: Gives an overview of Body Dysmorphic Disorder, including symptoms, warning signs, ways of detection, and treatment.
    ISBN 0-8239-2954-X
    1. Body dysmorphic disorder—Juvenile literature. [1. Body dysmorphic disorder.] I. Title. II. Series.
    RC569.5.B64W35   1999
    616.89—dc21   99-16747
                                                                  CIP
                                                                   AC

Manufactured in the United States of America

Contents

Introduction 6

1. What Is BDD? 13

2. The Causes of BDD 22

3. Who Is at Risk? 30

4. I Want to Look Normal 39

5. Is There Help for Me? 46

Glossary 58

Where to Go for Help 59

For Further Reading 61

Index 63

Introduction

Odds are that you are not familiar with body dysmorphic disorder. Most people have not even heard of it, let alone know what it is. Melissa, whose story you are about to read, is one of them.

Melissa

I can't stand it. I think about it all the time. How do you hide something as ugly as this? My face is too wide. It's not in proportion with the rest of my body, which is kind of small. When I see myself in the mirror, my head looks like a balloon on a string. I spend hours in front of the mirror just trying to fix it. I press my cheekbones with my hands and sometimes, for a minute or so, it seems like my face looks more normal. But then when I look at it again, or see it from a different angle, it's just as wide as before. And then I start pressing all over again.

Most days I don't even want to leave the house. I know that people stare at me. They must be thinking, "How awful! That poor girl with the huge head!" My friends act like they don't notice. They even compliment me sometimes and say things like, "I wish I had hair like yours, Melissa," or, "Your eyes are so gorgeous." But I know they're really looking at my head and thinking how huge and ugly it is. They're just trying to be nice and not hurt my feelings. Nobody will be honest with me about the problem. Anyway, I'm too embarrassed to bring it up myself.

The first time I noticed that my head had gotten really big was about a year ago. I had a date with this great-looking guy who I'd been wanting to go out with for a long time. I was kind of nervous and really wanted to look good. I went to the mall with a friend to buy a new outfit. I found an awesome dress and was trying it on in the dressing room when I got a really good look at myself in the mirror. I thought, "Oh, my God, why does my face look so wide?" It wasn't like I'd gained weight or anything. I mean, it wasn't like extra flesh, or chubby cheeks. It was just that my face was really wide—it made my head look huge, especially since the rest of my body is kind of petite.

My friend came in the dressing room and said, "Hey, the dress is perfect! God, you're so lucky. Matt is totally gorgeous."

Kind of casually, I asked her, "Do you think my head looks sort of big for the rest of my body?"

While others might see a beautiful face, she might look at her reflection and see ugliness and imperfection.

She said, "No way! Are you crazy? You're so beautiful, and you know it."

But I don't think she really took a good look. I ended up calling Matt and bailing out on the date. I just didn't want to deal with it. I couldn't stand the thought of him coming to pick me up and then realizing I looked like a freak.

Why couldn't I have some problem that I could change? I mean, if my nose was crooked or something I could have surgery, but there's nothing I can do about this. I try to wear my hair so that at least the sides of my face are covered up, but then my mom starts nagging me about it. "Don't cover up that pretty face, Melissa," she says.

When I mentioned to her once that I thought my head looked too big, she said something like, "Don't be silly. There's nothing wrong with you, Melissa. You inherited great bone structure."

Nobody understands how I feel. When I look in the mirror I see a monster.

Melissa is actually an attractive teen with above average looks, but her body image is distorted. When Melissa looks in the mirror, she can only focus on what she feels is an ugly and noticeable defect. Neither her mother nor her friends can convince Melissa that she looks normal. She is convinced that the image she sees in the mirror is what others see. She believes that her friends and family either don't understand or want to spare her feelings out of kindness or pity.

Melissa suffers from body dysmorphic disorder, or BDD. Like Melissa, most of us care about the way we look. We want to look our best. There are probably even certain aspects of our appearance that we wish we could change. There is nothing unusual about that. The problem begins when this dissatisfaction changes into a distorted and extremely negative image of ourselves. That is what is happening with Melissa, and it is the definition of BDD.

This book explains what happens when someone becomes excessively preoccupied with the way he or she looks. People who suffer from BDD feel intense emotional distress about some aspect of their appearance. It might be a "big" nose, or "weird" hair, or ears that "stick out." A person may focus on what he or she sees as a "hideous and ugly" defect, but friends and family may not see the defect at all or consider it only minimal.

What do you look like? What do you see when you look at yourself in a mirror? What do you think other people see when they look at you? The answers to these questions tell you about your body image, which is the way you see your body and the way you believe others see you. For some teens, normal concerns with body image become an obsession.

People with BDD may have such a negative body image that it interferes with their normal social inter-actions and relationships. "Who would want to be friends with someone who looks like me?" these people may ask. They often shun social activities and stay at home as much as possible.

BDD can lead to dangerous or self-destructive behavior. In some cases, a person may attempt to "correct" his or her perceived flaw. Self-correction may take the form of face-picking, or pulling at the skin with tweezers, or digging at the skin with the fingernails. Some people with BDD have even attempted to perform surgery on themselves when they could not persuade a plastic surgeon to help them.

People with BDD may also suffer from feelings of anxiety and depression. They may believe that suicide is the only way to stop the emotional pain and desperation they feel.

In the chapters to come, you'll learn more about BDD and what may cause people to develop negative and distorted images of themselves. Perhaps you have experienced some of these feelings. You may feel that you're "ugly" or that you have some horrible flaw in your appearance that you wish you could change. It may be hard for you to talk to anyone about it because, like Melissa, you are embarrassed to bring attention to it.

This book will help you to see that you are not alone. You will learn that there is help for the person who suffers from BDD. Finding out as much as you can about the disturbing and dangerous disorder known as BDD is the first step toward getting better.

When you catch a glimpse of yourself reflected in a window,
how do you feel about what you see?

Chapter 1

What Is BDD?

What do you really look like? Imagine walking into a room lined with fun-house mirrors at a carnival. Look closely at your face. In one mirror, your face is stretched long and thin. In another mirror, your face is short and wide. You open your mouth to smile, but the mirror changes it into a hideous red gash. Look at your whole body. As you pass by the mirrors, your body looks short and stumpy in one and long and lanky in another. What you see in the mirror is your image, all right, but one that has been distorted. You understand that these images are not what you really look like.

So how do you know what you do really look like? You know because everyone has an internal self-portrait. Your body image is this internal self-portrait—the way you see your body and the way you imagine your body looks to others.

Appearance Concerns: Are They Normal?

A recent survey showed that most people are not satisfied with the way they look. Every year in the United States, people spend millions of dollars on makeup, clothes, expensive haircuts, and even surgery in an attempt to improve their looks. They think that they would be happier if they looked better. Sometimes people are dissatisfied with one particular aspect of their appearance. Perhaps they think that their skin is not smooth enough or that their lips are too small.

For most people, such concerns about appearance are normal, in the sense that they occupy only a small part of their thoughts and do not greatly influence their behavior. But for the person who suffers from BDD, these concerns have gotten out of control. Physicians say that such a person's concern with his or her appearance has become excessive, disproportionate, or even obsessive.

People with BDD start to spend too much time thinking about what they consider a flaw or a deformity in their physical appearance. They may find that they are constantly worrying about the problem. Despite the emotional distress this causes them, some people are able to carry on a normal life. Even family members and close friends may never know how unhappy these people are.

But in extreme cases, BDD does interfere with a person's life. Gary tells his story in a darkened room because he does not want to be seen in normal light. He rarely leaves his house. When he does, he wears a cap pulled down to hide as much of his face as possible. Gary used to be a star soccer player, but he stopped playing the sport two years ago and cut all ties with his friends on the team. Last year he dropped out of school because he said he just could not face the stares of all the people who were horrified at his appearance.

Gary

This is really hard to talk about. I don't like to be seen in this much light. In fact, I think it's too bright in this room. I'd feel better if we could turn the lights down just a little more. Okay, that's better. It'll be easier for you to listen to me if you can't see me too clearly.

I have these craters on my face. It started a few years ago with just a couple of pimples. Then one morning I got up and looked in the mirror and my face was covered with pimples. I had never seen anything so disgusting in my life. I started squeezing them and my skin looked even worse. My face was red and splotchy all the time. It seemed like as soon as I got rid of one pimple, I would find even more in its place the next day.

My mom took me to a dermatologist, but she said it was just normal teenage acne and gave me a cream to rub on my face. It helped for a little while, but then the acne flared up again. Every day, I picked at the pimples. I would squeeze them and even try to dig them out with a nail file. Once I used sandpaper on my face until it bled. It seemed as if I couldn't keep my hands off my face. I heard about a treatment called dermabrasion, but my doctor wouldn't do it. She said my case was too mild— I think she just got tired of dealing with me.

I was always comparing my face to the faces of other people. I used to be a good soccer player, but I stopped playing because it seemed like all the other guys on the team had great skin. I knew they saw how ugly I was, and I believed they just wanted to keep me around to score more points.

After I quit playing, I left the house only to go to school. But it was taking me forever to get ready in the morning. I'd spend hours looking in the mirror and picking at the pimples. I was late almost every day. When I got to school, I couldn't concentrate because I was thinking about my face all the time. I knew that the way I looked was grossing people out. As soon as I turned sixteen, I quit school.

Sometimes late at night, I go outside and walk around in the dark. I wonder what's going to happen to me. I wonder about my future. But to be honest, I really don't think I have one. I don't see myself getting a job, or meeting a girl, marrying, having a family—I don't see myself doing any of the things that normal people do. I'm too ugly. I'd be better off dead.

Gary's dermatologist was right—he had a normal case of teenage acne. The cream she prescribed cleared it up. He had an occasional flare-up, which is normal, and in each case it was slight. But when Gary looked

When negative body image causes you to hide your face from the world, something is wrong.

in the mirror, he saw a very different picture. His negative body image was severe enough to cause him to quit soccer, drop out of school, and even entertain thoughts of suicide.

Who Has BDD?

Gary is not alone. Almost 5 million people—approximately 2 percent of the population of the United States—suffer from BDD. In most cases, the symptoms are first seen when the person is between the ages of fourteen and twenty. The disorder is equally common among men and women.

Doctors suspect that many cases of BDD go unreported. Often, people keep their worries and concerns a secret.

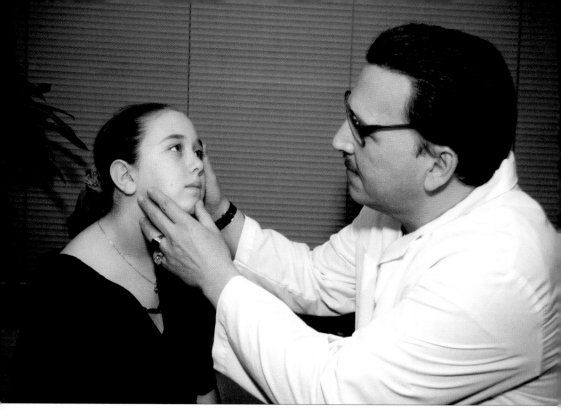

Doctors can tell you whether or not you have a physical problem, and can help you treat it if you do.

They may feel too ashamed or embarrassed to discuss their feelings with anyone, even close friends or family. When they do work up enough courage to talk about it to someone, they often feel as if they have not been understood. The friend may say, "I don't see anything wrong with you" and really mean it. But to the person with BDD, this may seem like a cop-out. He or she is likely to believe that the friend is trying to protect his or her feelings by not mentioning the defect or by minimizing it.

People with BDD are often not able to talk about the anxiety and depression they feel. Instead, they may spend their time looking for someone to "fix" the "deformity" they think they have. People with BDD often believe that if they can improve their appearance through plastic surgery or other means, then the anxiety and depression will go away.

In her book *The Broken Mirror*, Dr. Katherine A. Phillips explains that BDD is often misdiagnosed because the people who suffer from it seek treatment for a physical problem. Instead, what needs to be addressed are emotional or psychological issues. Phillips writes that "many people with BDD see dermatologists, plastic surgeons, and other physicians rather than mental health professionals. They search, usually unsuccessfully, for a cosmetic solution to a body-image problem."

Are Anorexia and Bulimia Forms of BDD?

Anorexia nervosa and bulimia nervosa are eating disorders that affect many teens. In some cases, the symptoms of these disorders are similar to or may even overlap the symptoms of BDD. All three disorders involve an extreme preoccupation with the body and its appearance. A teenager with anorexia nervosa may see herself as too fat when in fact she may be dangerously thin. Like the person who suffers from BDD, her body image is distorted.

But one very important difference is that a person with BDD usually looks normal and only imagines a defect. A person in an advanced stage of anorexia, by contrast, may appear completely emaciated. Often, the more abnormally thin the anorexic becomes, the more

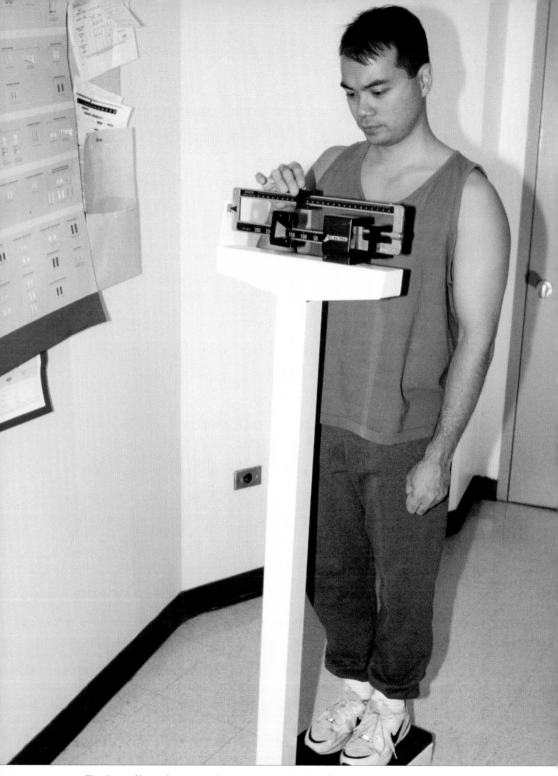

Eating disorders, such as anorexia, bulimia, compulsive eating, or compulsive exercise, can have symptoms very similar to those of BDD.

pleased he or she is. Even while family and friends are pleading with the person to seek help, the anorexic finally feels in full control and satisfied with the appearance of his or her body.

This is not the case for the person with BDD, who constantly feels distressed and dissatisfied with his or her body image. Because the person looks perfectly normal, family and friends often never know how miserable he or she feels.

Another important difference is the focus of the negative body image. A person with anorexia, bulimia, or another eating disorder is often concerned with overall body weight. Someone with BDD usually focuses on a specific body part. In most cases, the focus is on a facial feature.

There is still much to learn about each of these disorders. As research progresses, scientists and doctors are beginning to understand BDD better. For the person who suffers from it (or for the people who care about the sufferer), it is important to know that the disorder exists. Before a person can seek treatment for BDD, he or she must be aware of having a problem. Only then can this person begin to understand its symptoms and seek the necessary treatment.

In the next chapter, you will learn about some possible causes of BDD. What is society telling us about how we should look? What effect can those messages have on our body image? What role, if any, do those messages play in BDD?

Chapter 2

The Causes of BDD

If you asked a dozen people who have been diagnosed with BDD what they believe caused their symptoms, you would probably get a dozen different answers. Let's listen to three very common stories.

Terrina

When I was fourteen years old, my parents were going through a pretty nasty divorce, so they sent me upstate to stay with my cousin Jill for the summer. One day, as we changed into our swimsuits to take a dip in the pool, she blurted out, "Gosh, Terrina, I never realized how short your legs are!"

I looked in the mirror, and I realized she was right. I looked totally deformed. I couldn't get it out of my head for the rest of the summer. I refused to be seen in a swimsuit. I wore long pants, even on the hottest days.

People with BDD often remember moments when someone commented about their appearance as starting or adding to their negative body image.

That's when it started for me—that one comment from my cousin during the worst summer of my life when my family was breaking apart.

James

My older brother was the best at everything—sports, school, girls, you name it. My parents were so proud of him. I wanted to be like him, but I just couldn't cut it. I mean, I just wasn't him.

One day, I looked in the mirror and I saw that my ears were sticking out—sticking out much more than normal. Somehow, I started thinking that it was my stupid-looking ears that kept me from being like my brother. I figured

23

there was no use even trying anymore. How could anybody ever take me seriously? I looked like such a goon.

And it just kept getting worse. Every time I looked in the mirror—and I looked in the mirror a lot—it seemed like my ears were sticking out even more. I knew then that I could never be like my brother. I was destined to be the ugly duckling of the family.

Leilani

My hair had always been really long, but one summer I decided I wanted to wear it short. That summer this gorgeous model had her face plastered all over magazine covers, and her hairstyle was really short. I thought that if my hair was cut like hers, then I would look as good as she did.

In fact, I thought I looked a little bit like her anyway. So I took the magazine to the salon and told the guy to cut my hair just like that. It was a disaster. I started crying right there in the chair. The guy said, "What do you expect? Your hair is a different texture—it's thick. You could never get that exact same style. Besides, you don't look a thing like her. These scissors aren't a magic wand, you know!"

I wore a hat for months. I hated my hair. I hated my life. I hated everything, and it was all because I couldn't look like the girl on the magazine cover.

Possible Causes

So what causes BDD? Did Terrina's problem begin with her cousin's insensitive comment? Did the stress of

People with BDD tend to focus on a specific part of their body, such as their ears or their hair, and feel that these parts are abnormal and ugly.

her parents' divorce that summer have anything to do with it?

What about James? Did the fact that his brother seemed to be "perfect" at everything contribute to the development of his BDD symptoms?

And then there's Leilani. Could a picture on the cover of a magazine actually cause the kind of anxiety and depression that Leilani felt when she realized that she could not look like that?

We are constantly bombarded with images of attractive, almost "perfect" looking people in magazines, on television, and in movies. Is society sending a message that unless we have the "ideal" look of beauty, we aren't beautiful?

In fact, the actual causes of BDD are still unknown. Some researchers believe that biological factors, such as a chemical imbalance or another disturbance of the brain may be responsible for it. They think that a person's visual perception of himself or herself may become distorted as the result of such an imbalance or disturbance in the way the brain works. This disturbance causes the brain to misinterpret what the eyes are seeing.

It has also been suggested that psychological factors may play a role in the onset of BDD. Some people who develop the disorder have reported that they were frequently teased or subjected to hateful comments about some aspect of their appearance. An unhappy or traumatic experience in childhood is sometimes believed to contribute to BDD.

Other researchers have focused more on the role played by society and the media. Could such strong messages about the importance of attractiveness lead a person to develop an extreme preoccupation with his or her appearance?

Teens, especially, are likely to compare themselves with the images of the people they see in print, on television, and in film. This may be because young people are at a time in their lives when they are becoming concerned with their attractiveness to others, especially to members of the opposite sex. This culture's incessant focus on physical beauty, some researchers believe, may contribute to BDD. It is important to remember that for people who suffer from BDD, the goal is to look "normal." The question then becomes: What is normal?

Most scientists believe that there is no one cause of BDD. They believe that it results from a number of factors. They propose that genetics, psychological conflicts, and social and cultural pressures combine to lay the groundwork for the development of the disorder.

Much more research is needed before a single definite cause of BDD can be established. Like Terrina, James, and Leilani, some people who suffer from the problem often reach their own understanding of how it happened to them. But many others cannot explain what happened or even when they first began to notice the symptoms or that something was wrong. Each person's experience is unique. It is the task of the researchers to find some common theme in these

The beautiful faces we see in magazines and other media often contribute to our unrealistic ideas of beauty and perfection.

experiences that will help them understand more about this disorder.

In the meantime, it is important to know who may be at risk of developing BDD. In the next chapter, we will look at some of the early warning signs and symptoms of the disorder. We will also learn why it is so often misunderstood and misdiagnosed.

Chapter 3

Who Is at Risk?

Body dysmorphic disorder is extremely complex. There are as yet no definite answers about its cause. But certain behaviors may suggest that a person is at risk of developing BDD.

To learn whether you may be at risk of developing BDD, or whether you may already have developed some of the symptoms associated with the disorder, answer the following questions:

- Do you often check your appearance in mirrors or other reflecting surfaces, such as windows?
- Do you avoid mirrors because you dislike how you look?
- Do you frequently compare yourself to others and think that you look worse than they do?
- Do you often ask—or want to ask—others whether

you look okay, or whether you look as good as other people?

- Do you try to convince people that something is wrong with how you look, only to have them say they consider the problem nonexistent or minimal?
- Do you spend a lot of time grooming—for example, combing or arranging your hair, tweezing or cutting your hair, applying makeup, or shaving? Do you spend too much time getting ready in the morning, or do you groom yourself frequently during the day? Do others complain that you spend too much time in the bathroom?
- Do you pick at your skin, trying to make it look better?
- Do you try to cover or hide parts of your body with a hat, clothing, makeup, sunglasses, your hair, or other things? Is it painful to be around other people when you have not taken these protective steps?
- Do you often change your clothes, trying to find an outfit that covers or improves disliked aspects of your body? Do you take a long time selecting your outfit for the day, trying to find one that makes you look better?
- Do you try to hide aspects of your appearance by maintaining a certain body position—for example, turning your face away from others? Do you feel uncomfortable if you cannot be in your preferred position?

People with BDD sometimes do not want to leave the house until they have hidden or "fixed" a flaw in their appearance.

- Do you avoid having your picture taken because you think you look bad?
- Are you late for appointments or social engagements because you worry that you do not look right, or because you are trying to fix a "problem" with your appearance?
- Do you get depressed or anxious because of the way you look?
- Do you get frustrated or angry because of the way you look?
- Have you ever felt that life was not worth living because of your appearance?

The more yes answers that you give to these questions, the greater the risk that you might develop—or indeed already have—BDD. This determination is not one that you or anyone else can make alone, however. For an accurate evaluation, you need to see a doctor trained to diagnose BDD.

Carrie

I was sixteen when I was diagnosed with BDD. At first, my parents thought I was depressed about breaking up with my boyfriend. They thought I would get over it. What they didn't know was that I believed he broke up with me because of my facial hair.

For about a year I had noticed that hair kept growing and growing all over my face, but mostly on my chin and upper lip. I checked the mirror all the time to see if it

Are you ashamed of a feature of yours so much that you try to hide it in all situations?

had gone away. But it only seemed to get worse. I wanted to shave it off, but I was afraid it would grow back even coarser and darker than it already was. I started covering it with my hand when I was around people. I didn't like to be seen in bright light, and I refused to have my picture taken anymore because in one shot there was a dark shadow on my face—like a beard!

I kept canceling dates with Justin until finally he asked me what was going on. Even though it was one of the hardest things I ever did, I decided to tell him what was bothering me. He basically said, "You're crazy." At least, that's the message I got from him— well, that and the fact that he no longer wanted to date the bearded lady from the circus. I was so depressed that

Mom took me to see a doctor. She asked me a lot of questions about how I'd been feeling and what had been going on. That's how I found out that what I have has a name—it's BDD.

Body dysmorphic disorder usually starts in adolescence, but it may not be diagnosed for years. Some patients are too embarrassed or ashamed to talk about their symptoms with anyone. Sometimes people seek professional help for anxiety or depression but feel uncomfortable admitting concerns about their appearance. In some cases, doctors have never heard of BDD and misdiagnose the symptoms as those of some other disorder.

Carrie was lucky that she had a doctor who knew about body dysmorphic disorder and could accurately diagnose the problem. She felt better once she knew that what she had was a problem with a name—that she was not just "crazy." It also helped her to know that she was not the only one with this sort of disorder. Thanks to the accurate diagnosis by Carrie's doctor, she was able to get the help she needed.

Women and Men and BDD

For many reasons, people assume that BDD is more common among women than men. BDD shares some characteristics with the eating disorders anorexia and bulimia, which both affect far more women than men. In addition, the preoccupation of American society with physical appearance is directed much more strongly toward women. It is probably safe to say that women are much more likely than men to be judged on the basis of their physical appearance.

Since BDD concerns body image, it might seem logical that it would be a greater problem for women than men. But a recent study in *The Journal of Nervous and Mental Disease* indicated that just as many men as women are diagnosed with the disorder.

The study found many similarities in the way BDD affects men and women. In almost every case, the patients indicated that they began having the symptoms when they were teenagers.

The main difference that the report noted in the way men and women responded to BDD had to do with the body part that became the focus of the patient's preoccupation. Women expressed more concern about their hips, the size of their breasts, and the condition of their skin. Men's concerns centered more on their body build, hair loss, and the size of their genitals.

According to the study, the anxiety and depression that people feel as a result of this disorder seem to affect men and women to a similar degree. The study found the frequency of suicide attempts to be equal among patients of both sexes.

Is BDD Just Vanity?

How can you be so concerned with your looks all the time? You don't have hair on your face—you're crazy!

People with BDD are often misunderstood by friends and family as being vain.

What do you mean your ears "stick out"? You look perfectly normal!

Your legs aren't too short—you're just vain.

You're always looking in the mirror. You're always looking at yourself.

Don't be silly—you're very pretty, and you know it.

Everybody gets a pimple now and then—it's not the end of the world.

Don't be so shallow. Stop thinking about how you look all the time—it's not cool.

Those are typical comments that a person with BDD might hear from family and friends. It is very easy to mistake BDD for vanity. Since most people who suffer from the disorder look normal and may even be above average in attractiveness, concerns about their appearance may seem trivial.

Anyone who has felt the emotional pain and desperation associated with BDD understands that it is not a matter of vanity. In fact, it is the fear of being misunderstood or called "shallow" or "vain" that many times keeps the sufferer from talking to others about it.

In the next chapter, you will learn about certain behaviors and rituals that the person with BDD may engage in. You will also see how he or she sometimes involves family or friends in these obsessive behaviors. And you'll hear another story of someone with BDD— someone who just wants to "look normal."

Chapter 4

I Want to Look Normal

"I hated mirrors," Julianne says, "but I just couldn't stay away from them. Not just mirrors, but any kind of surface in which I could see my reflection and check my hair. I always felt that my hair was too flat. It stuck to my head like a cap, and it always looked dirty, no matter how many times I washed it. One day I washed my hair fifteen times, and it still didn't look right, but I couldn't stop washing it. I kept thinking, 'Okay, this time I'm going to get it right.' But it was never right.

"I was driving around with this guy once, and when we stopped to get gas, I ran inside to pick up a soda. I saw my reflection in the glass doors of the cooler where the sodas were kept. I don't know how long I stood there—just stuck to that place, looking at my hair, thinking, 'I'm completely disgusting! Why can't I look

Compulsive behavior such as excessive mirror checking is a sign that a person might have body dysmorphic disorder.

normal?' Then the guy came up behind me. I was totally embarrassed because he caught me looking at myself. I never went out with him again."

Many people with BDD engage in behaviors such as excessive mirror checking, hoping that when they look "this time," their "ugliness" will have disappeared or will not be as bad as they first thought. They hope that this will be the time that they look "normal."

When these people say, "I want to look normal," what are they really saying? What do they do to try to achieve that goal? What sort of behaviors do they engage in and why?

Many sufferers from BDD develop a need to perform

certain behaviors, or rituals, that they repeat over and over again. Doctors call this kind of behavior obsessive or compulsive. Julianne washed her hair fifteen times in one day. She said that she could not stop. People with BDD often feel that they have no control over these behaviors. The rituals take up such a huge part of the their day that they can get little else done.

People who engage in repetitive behavior, such as mirror-checking or hair-washing, do so in an attempt to control the level of stress and anxiety that they feel. Even if the behavior has never made them feel better before, they tell themselves that this time it will work. Or sometimes it works a little bit, for a short period of time. When it wears off and the stress and anxiety returns, they repeat the procedure.

Involving Family and Friends

Sometimes people with BDD involve family members or friends in their compulsive behaviors. In addition to mirror-checking and hair-washing, Julianne developed the compulsion to question her mother. At first, she was hoping for reassurance about the way her hair looked. But as her disorder developed, Julianne found that she simply could not stop, no matter what answers she received. Even though her mother never had the answers that Julianne looked for, she continued to ask the same kinds of questions. Julianne would even get angry with her mother for not saying what she wanted to hear.

Julianne's Mother

It always started in the morning, when Julianne was getting ready for school. She'd ask, "Does my hair look okay?" I would, of course, answer, "Yes, it looks very nice," and it was the truth—she's always had great hair. Julianne is truly a beautiful young woman, and I would tell her so.

But it never stopped there. She would go back to her room, or to the bathroom, and then come out and ask all over again, "Are you sure it looks okay? Don't you think it looks flat?" She would turn around so that I could see her hair from all sides. Then she'd look at her reflection in the windowpane. Once again, I'd reassure her that her hair looked fine. But she would go back to the bathroom and wash her hair all over again.

She was late to school almost every day. And many times I was late to work because Julianne would insist that I stay with her until she could get her hair to look "just right." There was nothing I could say. If I complimented her too much, she would say that I didn't mean it and that I was only trying to "rush her" so we could get out of the house faster. If I didn't say anything, then she would accuse me of being ashamed of her for being so "ugly." It was a no-win situation.

Parents often feel they are in a "no-win" situation with teens who have BDD. Julianne's mother wanted to help her daughter. She wanted to reassure her that her hair was fine and that she was a beautiful girl. But this

A person with BDD might wash their hair over and over again hoping that the next time they wash it, it will finally look acceptable.

was never enough for Julianne, nor would it ever be.

When faced with the emotional pain and desperation of a loved one struggling with BDD, friends and family want more than anything to help make it go away. They usually think they can do this through reassurance or by "explaining" it away.

In other words, when Julianne gets upset about her hair and seeks reassurance, her mother tries to "explain" to Julianne that she is a beautiful young woman and that she has great hair. She hopes that by pointing out the truth to her daughter, it will be possible to convince her that there's nothing wrong with her appearance. Unfortunately, reassurance alone is not enough to make the symptoms go away.

Like others who suffer from BDD, Julianne believes that the time will come when her mother will finally be able to convince her that everything is okay. So she continues to ask the same questions over and over again:

Are you sure it looks okay? Are you just saying that? I look terrible, don't I? I'm ugly. I'm a monster—go ahead, admit it. You know that I'm ugly. Why don't you just say so? Why don't you tell the truth?

It is heartbreaking for a parent to hear such words. It's heartbreaking for a friend or a brother or sister to hear such words. And the heartache only gets worse when the person who is speaking the words cannot understand that what he or she is dealing with is a disorder.

Although sufferers of BDD rarely believe the affirming words of friends or family, they often repeatedly ask for their opinions about their appearance anyway.

That is why people with BDD so often feel great relief after being diagnosed with the disorder. At last, they feel, there is a reason, some explanation for their behavior. There is some cause for their anxiety and depression and for the struggle that they have been undergoing. And the greatest relief of all is learning that something can be done about the disorder to make it better. So if you are experiencing the symptoms of BDD, or if someone you know is, be aware that there are ways to get help.

Chapter 5

Is There Help for Me?

For many people, admitting that they have a problem is one of the most difficult things for them to do. People with body dysmorphic disorder have low self-esteem, or sense of self-worth. To begin the process of admitting that a concern about their appearance has become something more—a problem that needs to be addressed—can be embarrassing and difficult. They may be afraid of being called "shallow" or "vain" and that no one can ever really understand what is going on. They may fear that other people will think they are "crazy" or not normal. But there are people who will understand and steer them to the help they need.

Whom to Tell?

Think about all the people you know. To whom do you feel really comfortable talking? Who do you think will really listen? You may feel more at ease talking to a parent, or a brother or sister. Or maybe you feel closer to a teacher or a counselor from your school or your religious organization.

Whomever you decide to talk to, it will help if you think about and plan what you want to say. It will also help if you realize that at first you may not get the kind of response you are hoping for. It can be as hard for someone to respond to you in a constructive way as it can be for you to reach out and talk to someone about your problem. The person you talk to may need some time to figure out how to help you. He or she may need time to learn about BDD or to find out how to get you the help that you need.

Kemal

I'd been dealing with the problem for about a year before I finally talked to somebody. Man, I almost gave up after telling my brother that I thought something was wrong with me. I thought my body was too small, and that it made me look weak. And what was even more scary was that I started thinking it was getting smaller and smaller. There was one time when I was home by myself and I freaked out because I started thinking that I was gonna fade away, like completely disappear.

When I told my brother, he laughed at me. "Yeah, Kemal, you are too small, you little sissy." I was upset, but I didn't want him to see me cry. I walked out of the room, and he went back to watching television. He teased

It's important to talk with someone about your feelings in order
to overcome body dysmorphic disorder.

me for a few more days, but finally he moved on to something else. Meantime, I'm feeling worse and worse, thinking that there's nobody for me to talk to.

Then one day I'm sitting out on the bleachers at school by myself. It was after football practice, and I thought everybody had gone home. But Coach Ben walked over and sat down beside me.

"What's going on, kid?" he asked. And that was it for me. Somehow I knew that he would listen. I told him the whole story. He listened to everything and asked me some questions. And then he told me that I wasn't alone. He said lots of people feel that there's something wrong with the way they look and that sometimes those feelings get out of hand. He said that there was help and that he would stick with me and make sure I got through everything okay.

Kemal's coach listened to him. He did not rush to conclusions, he did not make judgments, and he did not think that Kemal was "crazy" for thinking that something was wrong with him. Coach Ben let Kemal know that there was help for him.

Planning the "Big Talk"

Once you have decided that you need to do something about the way you're feeling, the first step is to tell someone else. No one gets over BDD alone. You can start to regain control of your life by taking control over whom you tell and how you tell them.

Think about whom you want to talk to. Once you

have decided who it should be, then make sure that you pick a good time—a good time for you to talk, and a good time for the person to listen. Both of you are going to want some privacy while you talk, and you will not want a lot of interruptions. You need to have this person's full attention.

It might even be good to schedule a time and place to talk. That doesn't mean that you have to make a big deal out of it; just say something like, "Hey, I need to talk to you about something. Alone. Can you do it?" Then ask when would be a good time and where would be a good place. That helps the other person understand right away that this is a serious matter for you.

When it comes time for you to talk, you may find it very hard to start. You may not know where to begin. You may be afraid of saying too much, of not saying enough, or of somehow not saying the right thing. It may help if you write down a few things in advance. In describing the way you feel, focus on the things that you think are most important. There's no one "right thing" that you have to say. What you need to do is to make the other person understand how you feel.

At first, the person may try to convince you that nothing is wrong with the way you look. You may hear things like, "You're a beautiful person. There's nothing wrong with the way you look. I've always wished I could look like you."

You must keep in mind the point that you want to get across: The "thoughts" you are having need to be changed, and you cannot do it by yourself. It may be hard to make someone understand that what you see in the mirror is different from what others see when they look at you. The point is not so much whether your feelings about your body are right or wrong, accurate or inaccurate. What you need to communicate is that these thoughts about your body are beginning to take over your life, and that this is making you increasingly unhappy.

Even though you plan what you are going to say, and choose whom you want to say it to, you may feel that the person just does not seem to understand. Don't give up. Give the person a chance; try again. Maybe he or she wants to help, but does not know how. Or maybe the person just cannot understand. Do not give up. If you must, find someone else to talk to.

Talking to someone is well worth the difficulty. Once you have done it, you will probably feel a great sense of relief. Teens who suffered from BDD often report that it was not until they told somebody that they felt—for the first time—any sense of hope.

Getting Professional Help

The next step in seeking the help you need is to get an accurate diagnosis from a trained health care professional. Even though much research is being done on BDD, some health professionals may not be familiar with the disorder.

A good place to start is with your family doctor,

especially if you have not had a physical examination in a while. Your doctor may be able to recommend a therapist for you. If your family has health insurance, you may be able to find a qualified therapist through your insurance coverage.

It is important to be as open and communicative as you possibly can with your doctor or therapist. Ask questions, and do not hold back anything about what you have been going through. Your doctor or therapist needs to know as much as possible about you if he or she is to be able to provide the help you need. Taking an active role in planning your recovery is the most important step you can take toward getting well.

What Kind of Treatment Will I Get?

A number of treatment options are available to people with BDD. Keeping the lines of communication open will help you and your family make the best decision about the type of treatment you receive.

In individual therapy, a patient meets with a therapist for one-on-one sessions. It is important to remember that the therapist wants to help you. For him or her to do that, you must be honest about your feelings and your concerns. Many people who have had therapy say that one of the most difficult hurdles to overcome was the initial embarrassment and shame of discussing their symptoms with their therapist. They may have lived for years trying to hide or cover up what they saw as their "ugliness." It was not easy for them to

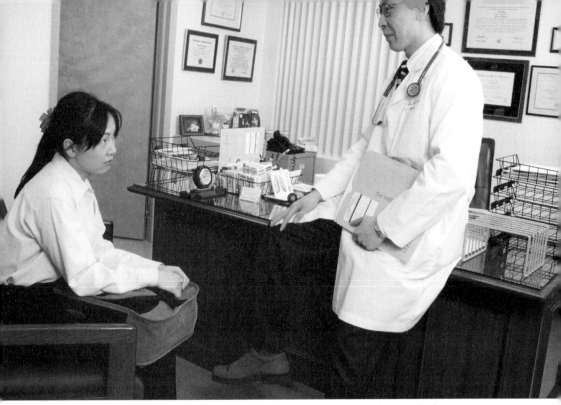

A medical doctor may decide to prescribe medication to help you recover from anxiety or depression.

draw attention to their perceived defect with a complete stranger.

But remember, the therapist is there to help—not to judge. Therapists have been trained to help people talk about their problems. A skilled therapist understands that talking about symptoms can be uncomfortable. Your therapist is trained to ask questions that will help you understand yourself better. One of the most important things that a therapist does is help you overcome negative attitudes and beliefs about yourself.

In family therapy, a trained therapist works with the patient and the family to help everyone better understand BDD. The therapist helps the family to learn ways to cope with feelings they may have during the treatment process. As we have learned, the person who suffers from BDD often involves family members by seeking reassurance about his or her appearance or by blaming them for his or her unhappiness. The family is often drawn into the rituals and behaviors of BDD.

In some cases, a medication may be prescribed to assist in the treatment of BDD. A number of medications, particularly antidepressants, are currently being studied to determine their effectiveness in treating this disorder. Some people have reported that medication and therapy together have been helpful in relieving their anxiety and depression. They also say that the medication helps control their obsessive thoughts.

If your doctor prescribes medication, be sure to ask about the drug. Find out what the medication is expected to do and what side effects may be involved.

It is important for your treatment for you to realize that you have a say in what happens to you. Ask questions whenever you are not sure about what is being done. Many issues will come up during treatment that you will need to deal with. Each time you take control and meet these issues, you are making bold steps in your recovery process.

No treatment plan works equally well for everyone. A time may come when you feel that you are not making the progress you should. If this happens, it might be wise to step back and take a look at the treatment plan that has been established. You may suggest changes, or you may simply say that you do not think the present treatment is giving you the kind of help you need.

Throughout the period of your recovery, it will be important for you to speak up and let your feelings be known. You did not develop BDD overnight, and you cannot recover overnight. Making a commitment to yourself during this time of healing is one of the most important things you will ever do for yourself.

In chapter one, we read Gary's painful story. He described a life lived in seclusion because he could not bear to be seen. He walked the streets at night, wondering about his future, believing that his "ugliness" meant that there would be no future for him. He thought about suicide as a way out of the pain and hopelessness he felt. How is Gary now?

Gary: One Year Later

Man, this thing called BDD. When I think back to a year ago, I can hardly believe that guy was me. It was my mom who finally insisted that I get help. She went to the library and started looking up stuff that described what was going on. She talked to the librarian, and they found a book about BDD.

She came home and told me about it, but I refused to listen. It was my problem, I told her. I was ugly and that was it—there wasn't anything in a book that could change that fact.

But one morning when she was at work, I picked up the book and started reading it. At first it was hard to

With the support of family and friends, and accurate information about the condition, people with BDD can lead happy, confident lives.

believe that there were other people in the world who felt like me. It got me thinking, "Maybe it's not just me— maybe I'm not that ugly. Maybe there's something wrong with the way I see myself." Was it possible that other people didn't see huge craters in my face when they looked at me? Could this BDD thing be for real?

I finally talked to my mom about it, and the next day we made an appointment with a doctor. I've been in therapy for a year now, and I understand that what I saw in the mirror was not the real me. I saw this grotesque monster who was not fit for anything—not even fit to live. I wanted to kill the monster so that I would stop hurting.

There are still times when my thoughts start to get away from me. It might be a quick glance in the mirror, and I start to see myself the old way. But now I know what to do about it. I stay calm. I feel that I'm the one who controls my life now, and not the monster in the mirror that I used to see. It feels good to be alive.

Glossary

anorexia nervosa   An eating disorder character-
ized by an obsessive desire to lose weight. Most
people who suffer from anorexia nervosa are young
women in their teens and early twenties.

antidepressant   Medication used in the treatment
of clinical depression. Some antidepressants are
used to treat other conditions as well, such as
obsessive-compulsive disorder.

anxiety   A state of intense apprehension, uncertainty,
and fear resulting from the anticipation of a threat-
ening event or situation.

body image   The way you see yourself and how
you think others see you.

bulimia   A disorder in which overeating alternates
with self-induced vomiting.

deformity   A misshapen body part or feature.

depression   A state of extreme sadness, dejection,
and hopelessness.

obsession   A recurring thought that is difficult to
dismiss.

ritual   A repetitive behavior performed to prevent or
reduce stress or anxiety.

self-esteem   One's sense of self-worth.

Where to Go for Help

American Anorexia/Bulimia Association (AABA)
165 West 46th Street, Suite 1108
New York, NY 10036
(212) 575-6200
Web site: members.aol.com/AmAnBu
E-mail: amanbu@aol.com

American Self-Help Clearinghouse
http://www.cmhc.com/selfhelp
Provides links to more than a thousand self-help and support groups on-line.

Anorexia Nervosa and Related Disorders
P.O. Box 5102
Eugene, OR 97405
(541) 344-1144

Council on Size and Weight Discrimination
P.O. Box 305
Mount Marion, NY 12456
(914) 679-1206
Fax: (914) 679-1206

Largesse: The Network for Size Esteem
P.O. Box 9404
New Haven, CT 06534
(203) 787-1624
Fax: (203) 787-1624
e-mail: 75773.717@compuserve.com
Provides individuals with resources to help develop a more positive body image.

Obsessive Compulsive Foundation
P.O. Box 70
Milford, CT 06460-0070
(203) 878-5669
Web site: http://www.ocfoundation.org
The foundation can also provide information on support groups for BDD.

Teen Advice On-line
Web site: http://www.teenadviceonline.org
Provides support for teenage problems through a network of peers around the globe.

For Further Reading

Beckelman, Laurie. *Body Blues*. New York: Crestwood House, 1994.

Branden, Nathaniel. *How to Raise Your Self-Esteem.* New York: Bantam Books, 1987.

Burby, Liza. *Bulimia Nervosa: The Secret Cycle of Bingeing and Purging.* New York: Rosen Publishing Group, 1998.

Cash, Thomas, Ph.D. *The Body Image Workbook: An 8-Step Program for Learning to Like Your Looks.* Oakland, CA: New Harbinger Publications, 1997.

———.*What Do You See When You Look in the Mirror? Helping Yourself to a Positive Body Image.* New York: Bantam, 1995.

Cooke, Kaz. *Real Gorgeous: The Truth About Body and Beauty.* New York: W.W. Norton, 1996.

Davis, Brangien. *What's Real, What's Ideal: Overcoming a Negative Body Image.* New York: Rosen Publishing Group, 1999.

Graff, Cynthia Stamper, Janet Eastman, and Mark C. Smith. *Bodypride: An Action Plan for Teens.* Glendale, CA: Griffin Publishing, 1998.

Hillman, Carolynn. *Love Your Looks: How to Stop Criticizing and Start Appreciating Your Appearance.* New York: Simon & Schuster, 1996.

Hutchinson, Marcia G. *Transforming Body Image: Learning to Love the Body You Have.* Freedom, CA: Crossing Press 1988.

Ignoffo, Matthew, Ph.D. *Self-Confidence.* New York: Rosen Publishing Group, 1996.

Jukes, Mavis. *It's a Girl Thing: How to Stay Healthy, Safe, and in Charge.* New York: Knopf, 1996.

Markham, Ursula. *Creating a Positive Self-Image: Simple Techniques to Transform Your Life.* Rockport, MA: Element, 1995.

McCoy, Kathy, and Charles Wibbelsman, M.D. *Life Happens: A Teenager's Guide to Friends, Failure, Sexuality, Love.* New York: Berkley, 1996.

Newman, Leslea. *Some Body to Love: A Guide to Loving the Body You Have.* Chicago, IL: Third Side Press, 1991.

Phillips, Katherine A., M.D. *The Broken Mirror: Understanding and Treating Body Dysmorphic Disorder.* New York: Oxford, 1996.

Smith, Erica. *Anorexia Nervosa: When Food Is the Enemy.* New York: Rosen Publishing Group, 1999.

Index

A

adolescence, 35
anorexia nervosa, 21, 35
    defined, 19
    differences between, 19-20
anxiety, 11, 18, 26, 33, 35-36, 41, 45
appearance, 10, 11, 14, 19, 21, 26, 30-
    33, 36, 38, 46
attitude, 53
attractiveness, 26

B

body dysmorphic disorder
    ages affected, 17
    by gender, 17, 35-36
    causes of, 22-29
    defined, 10
    early warning signs of, 29, 30-33
    examples of, 6, 15, 22-24, 33, 39,
        42, 47, 55
    percentage of population
        affected, 17, 29, 31-33, 35-36,
        45
    treatment of, 21, 52-55
body image, 9-10, 17, 19, 21, 36
biological factors
    chemical imbalance, 26
bulimia nervosa, 19, 21, 35

C

communication, 46, 51-52
control, 49, 54, 57
cultural pressures, 27

D

deformity, 14, 18
depression, 11, 18, 26, 33-36, 45
dermabrasion, 16
dermatology, 15, 19
desperation, 11, 38, 44
dissatisfaction, 10, 14, 21

E

embarrassment, 7, 11, 18, 35, 52
emotional pain, 10-11, 14, 38, 44
evaluation, 33

F

family, 9, 14, 18, 21, 37-38, 41, 44, 53
friends, 7, 9, 14, 18, 21, 37-38, 41,
    44

G

genetics, 27

H

help, 46-57

M

media
    magazines, 24, 26-27
    movies, 27
    television, 27
medication
    antidepressants, 54
mental-health professionals, 19, 52
misdiagnosis, 27

N
negative images, 10-11, 17, 21

O
obsession, 10, 14, 38
obsessive-compulsive, 41
P
Phillips, Dr. Katherine A., 19
physical beauty, 27
plastic surgery, 11, 14, 19
psychological factors, 26

R
reassurance, 41-42, 44
recovery, 52, 54-55
relationships, 10
research, 21, 27, 36, 51
rituals, 38, 41

S
self-correction, 11
self-destructive behavior, 11

self-esteem, 46
self-portrait, 13
self-worth, 46
shame, 18, 35, 52
social activities, 10, 33
society, 21, 26-27, 35
stress, 24, 41
suicide, 11, 17, 36

T
teenagers, 10, 19, 27, 36, 42, 51
therapy
    family, 53
    individual, 52

V
vanity, 36-38, 46

About the Author

Pamela Walker is an editor and freelance writer in New York City.

Photo Credits

Cover photo by Brian T. Silak.
P. 20 by John Bentham; pp. 45, 56 by Ira Fox; p. 53 by Maike Schultz;
all other photos by Brian T. Silak.